Shock the

Clock:

Time Management for Writers and Other Creatives

JEANETTE LEVELLIE
Drawings by Ron Levellie

Lighthouse Publishing
of the Carolinas

SHOCK THE CLOCK BY JEANETTE LEVELLIE
Published by Lighthouse Publishing of the Carolinas
2333 Barton Oaks Dr., Raleigh, NC, 27614

ISBN: 978-1-941103-51-7
Copyright © 2015 by Jeanette Levellie
Cover design by Elaina Lee
Interior design by AtriTeX Technologies P Ltd

Available in print from your local bookstore, online, or from the publisher at: www.lighthousepublishingofthecarolinas.com

For more information on this book and the author visit: www.jeanettelevellie.com

Brought to you by the creative team at Lighthouse Publishing of the Carolinas: Shonda Savage, Carolyn Boyles, Brian Cross

Library of Congress Cataloging-in-Publication Data
Levellie, Jeanette *Shock the Clock*
Shock the Clock Jeanette Levellie 1st ed.

Printed in the United States of America

Praise for
Shock the Clock

"Jeanette Levellie's book, *Shock the Clock*, is perfect for delivering time tips to writers like me. I'm a type A++ combo choleric/sanguine personality who gets asked all the time how I get so much done. But I feel like there's so much more to do. Jeanette helped me find those tips to beat my schedule challenges based on my sense of drive and desire to have fun. She'll help you, too, and you'll smile the entire time."

~Angela Breidenbach
author/speaker and President of the Christian
Authors Network

"I've never believed in 'time management,' but I've always believed in *self* management. So, I'm taking time to recommend *Shock the Clock*, Jeanette's warm, wise, and witty book on managing yourself while carving out chunks of time to be creative. And it's short, so you *do* have time to read it!"

~James N. Watkins
award-winning author, speaker, and clock-shocker

"*Shock the Clock* by Jeanette Levellie offers a great combination of time management tips, action steps, and wisdom. Her humorous and down-to-earth style engages readers, offering ready-to-use, seasoned advice with a delightful and heartfelt dose of encouragement."

~Karen Lange
freelance writer and editor, author, and online writing instructor

"Excellent crash course in time management: I found much that I could use."

~Donn Taylor
author of *Lightning on a Quiet Night*, *Rhapsody in Red*, *Deadly Additive,* and *The Lazarus File*

"Filled with practical suggestions and lots of wisdom, *Shock the Clock* is the perfect tool to make the most of your writing and marketing hours."

~Alice J. Wisler
author of *Rain Song*

"As a mother of five, finding time to write is no easy task. But using tips from Jeanette Levellie's *Shock the Clock* has definitely helped me to be more productive and get more writing done. I especially loved that the tips were designed for my specific personality type."

~Diane Stark
author of over 30 *Chicken Soup for the Soul* stories

Table of Contents

Acknowledgments 7

Dedication...8

Foreword 9

Chapter 1 What Works for Your Unique
Personality?...11

Chapter 2 The 10 D's of Time Management........17

Chapter 3 Minutes Count 29

Chapter 4 Forty Time Management Tips
and Secrets...31

Chapter 5 Confessions of a Clutter
Hypocrite 39

Chapter 6 Top Ten Time Thieves That
Attack Writers 43

Chapter 7 Ask an Expert.......................................47

Recommended Reading and Websites 57

Works Cited 61

Acknowledgments

Here comes the part where I get to shout
For all the folks who've helped me out.
No, I could never do without
These VIPs, I have no doubt.

Kevin: For your example of prioritizing tasks but mostly your example of Jesus.

Diana Flegal: For sharing the concept of baby steps and for believing in my words.

Mom: For teaching me to clean as I cook (even though I rarely cook these days).

Diana Savage: For your wisdom, editing expertise, and nurturing friendship.

Eddie Jones and Cindy Sproles: For your confidence in me, again.

Marie and Ron: For teaching me that people trump tasks, and for helping me laugh at myself. You are the best daughter and son ever.

Jenessa, Daniel, and Grace: For being three splendid reasons to manage my time—so I can spend more with you. You guys make my heart sing!

God, the One and Only: For Your unending love and mercy toward this messy redhead.

Dedication

To Jesus Christ, The Timeless One

I love You more than

Kitties, Dark Chocolate, and Laughing Babies

Foreword

I was not born organized. My crib was messy. I did not eat on schedule. All my puzzles had missing pieces. And that was just last week.

But I learned some tricks and secrets from people who had tidy cribs and never lost puzzle pieces. I hung out with some of them—my husband in particular—and let them rub off on me. Now, I am neater than he is, and that makes him mad. But I digress.

I started writing when my kids were one and three years old, respectively, took a sabbatical of ten years, then started up again when they were teens. *All* my writing has been accomplished while raising kids, homeschooling, working full-time outside my home, and serving as a pastor's wife. I've published hundreds of columns, articles, greeting card verses, stories, and two books.

So … you can do this, too.

Chapter 1
What Works for Your Unique Personality?

*I*n the following charts, I've tried to help you discover where your personality fits based on the four classic types: Sanguine, Choleric, Phlegmatic, or Melancholy. Of course, you won't match exactly in only one category—everyone is a mixture. But your dominant traits will help you analyze how you view life, relate to others, and manage—or not—your time.

When you realize it's okay to be mellow (phlegmatic) or strong (choleric) or goofy (sanguine) or sensitive (melancholy), you'll be free to find the unique, blissful path God wants for you. Your time management won't look like Writer A, Editor B, or Poet C, because you're not wired like them. You need to manage tasks according to your distinctive personality strengths and challenges.

Become comfortable with the awesome, precious individual God designed you to be! As you do, you'll realize whatever changes the Lord prompts you to make to better manage your time spring from His deep love. He knows you long to touch more lives with your writing, produce quality work, and waste less time. He wants that for you, too.

So let Him lead you to be the best *you* possible, in the style that suits your personality, not emulating anyone else. Then every achievement will be to His glory, and you will feel Him smile.

Sanguine (*The Fun Ones*)

Your Strengths	Using Your Strengths to Achieve Your Goals & God's Plans
◊ Find the fun way to accomplish tasks ◊ Love to bring out the best in others ◊ Have the gift of gab ◊ Get excited over little things ◊ Are full of bright ideas ◊ Can change plans in an instant ◊ Are great at multitasking ◊ Enjoy people	◊ Reward yourself for goals met ◊ Get others involved by delegating ◊ Develop a speaking ministry ◊ Share your ideas to help others succeed ◊ Read your work aloud for greater clarity of thought ◊ See your writing as a way to help others grow
Your Unique Challenges	**Overcoming Your Challenges**
◊ The gift of gab can get you into trouble if you exaggerate ◊ As a people pleaser, you often over commit ◊ You tend to clutter your workspace ◊ Impulsive and impatient, you can't stand tedium or details ◊ In love with fun, you can be unrealistic about how life should be ◊ You'd rather start something new than sludge through to finish	◊ Listen more than you talk, especially to God ◊ Learn to say no to requests you haven't prayed about ◊ Reduce distractions by simplifying your environment ◊ Take your time and be thorough ◊ Give yourself permission to do boring tasks ◊ Commit only to what you *know* you can finish

Choleric (*The Fearless Ones*)

Your Strengths	Using Your Strengths to Achieve Your Goals & God's Plans
<ul><li>Can accomplish much work in a short time</li><li>Are organized and efficient</li><li>Have great leadership skills</li><li>Can make decisions quickly</li><li>Are goal-oriented</li><li>Have excellent ideas for growth</li><li>Know how to surround yourself with people to help you achieve your goals</li></ul>	<ul><li>Make lists and charts for short-term and long-term goals</li><li>Keep workspace clutter-free</li><li>Deal with each issue as it comes up</li><li>Don't look back, but forward</li><li>Delegate</li><li>Teach others what you know, to perpetuate your wisdom</li></ul>
Your Unique Challenges	**Overcoming Your Challenges**
<ul><li>Tend to forge ahead on your own</li><li>Think there is only one right way</li><li>Set standards too high, then berate yourself when you fail</li><li>Let achievements and goals override relationships</li><li>Tempted to think your way is the only way</li><li>Prone to workaholism</li></ul>	<ul><li>Listen to the Lord's voice</li><li>Practice flexibility</li><li>Eliminate unrealistic expectations</li><li>Focus on people rather than tasks</li><li>Be open to others' ideas</li><li>Give yourself permission to relax</li></ul>

Phlegmatic (*The Friendly Ones*)

Your Strengths	Using Your Strengths to Achieve Your Goals & God's Plans
♥ Great listener ♥ Easy to get along with ♥ Easy to please ♥ Natural peacemaker ♥ Enjoy serving others ♥ Flexible ♥ Fun ♥ Not easily upset or ruffled	♥ Listen to God's leading ♥ View your writing as a service to others ♥ Use rewards to motivate yourself ♥ Choose friends who are well-disciplined and learn their ways ♥ Find the simplest way to accomplish a task ♥ Break jobs down into bite-sized pieces ♥ Can work well under pressure
Your Unique Challenges	**Overcoming Your Challenges**
♥ Need outside motivation ♥ Easily distracted; hard to focus ♥ Want others to take responsibility ♥ Like to please, but see no need to follow through on commitments ♥ Led by feelings and others ♥ Live for the moment, procrastination causes stress in reaching goals	♥ Set the timer and work until it dings ♥ Eliminate distractions ♥ Refuse to make excuses ♥ Say yes only if you can follow through ♥ Set baby step goals and add a bit each week ♥ Do the right thing, even if your feelings want to play and rest ♥ Have an accountability partner

Melancholy (*The Feeling Ones*)

Your Strengths	Using Your Strengths to Achieve Your Goals & God's Plans
✓ Attention to detail ✓ Creative, artistic ✓ Do well with routines ✓ Faithful friend ✓ Orderly, organized ✓ Enjoy researching ✓ Feel deeply	✓ Make lists and check off items as you accomplish them ✓ Prioritize according to importance or deadlines ✓ Break down big projects into small pieces ✓ Do your work thoroughly ✓ Use research to enhance your work
Your Unique Challenges	**Overcoming Your Challenges**
✓ Take life and self too seriously ✓ Perfectionism can keep you from finishing projects ✓ Find security in things, so can lean toward cluttered environment ✓ Worries, wishes, and "what ifs" ✓ Get bogged down in detail ✓ Overly hard on self	✓ Smile and laugh more often ✓ Learn to say "It's good enough" ✓ Eliminate clutter ✓ Live in the present—don't waste time on regrets or worry ✓ Focus on the overall picture ✓ Forgive yourself if you aren't perfect

Chapter 2
The 10 D's of Time Management

1. Delight Yourself in the Lord

Put God first, and He will collaborate with you to help you meet your goals. To work smarter rather than harder and accomplish more in the hours God gives us, we need the Lord's wisdom more than we need new systems, tools, and man's ideas.

Based on your personality, delighting yourself in the Lord will look different from your neighbors' ways. What ways have you found that best suit you?

_____

_____

2. Do Away with Fear

Fear of failure paralyzes us. Fear of success keeps us in a rut. *The results are the same!*

Identify your fears, then take each one to the throne of grace, and ask God to deliver you. Find Scriptures that assure you of God's protection. Which one applies the most to a fear related to writing or publishing?

_____

_____

3. De-clutter and De-junk

Taking care of clutter takes time away from your calling. The simpler your environment, the more time you have to do what you enjoy.

A. What types of clutter challenge you most?

_____

B. How can you help yourself stay free of clutter?

_____

4. Discipline Your Flesh

No is not a four-letter word. Say it with grace and dignity. We not only need to say "no" to wasting time, but also to the unrealistic expectations of those around us. If you, like me, are a people pleaser by nature, you may need to ask the Lord to bolster your confidence and seek His will above others' opinions.

What people and/or activities do you need to say "no" to?

_____

_____

_____

5. Divide Writing and Marketing Time

If no one knows you, your writing lacks an audience. If you don't write, your audience will go elsewhere.

For beginning writers, split writing and marketing time 80%/20%.

For intermediate writers, experts recommend a 50%/50% split.

In the three months after a book's release, a 20%/80% split ensures good promotion.

What is your current writing/marketing time ratio?

_____

How can you creatively use your time to find the balance you need?

_____

_____

_____

6. Delegate

If you allow others to help, you affirm their part in the team, and the finish line comes sooner.

Ways to delegate:

◊ Enlist family members for researching, accepting friends on Facebook©, cooking, running errands, and cleaning.

◊ Consider hiring help. If you can't afford to hire help, perhaps a family member, church member, friend, or neighbor would be willing. Your health is worth it.

◊   Listen and be open to others' ideas.

If you are not comfortable delegating, choose a baby step to begin taking pressure off yourself.

---

7. Decide What's Important
If you knew you had only two more years to live, what would you spend your time doing?

How to decide what's important:

⇒   Ask the Lord to direct your steps and help you focus on your strengths.

⇒   Don't waste time trying to be someone else.

⇒   Identify what you enjoy doing most.

_____

_____

_____

_____

8. Dance and Sing—Take Time to Play

Recreation means "to impart fresh life to, to create anew." The mind creates best when we allow time each day to relax and divert our attention away from work. Thomas Edison often stretched out on a couch and let his mind wander as a way to solve problems. The best performers in art, music, athletics, business, and writing are not workaholics. They have learned recreation plays an effective role in their success.

Ways to play that refresh are different for everyone.

➤ Laughter is a form of exercise.

➤ It's okay to do nothing for an hour or a day.

➤ Enjoying nature renews your soul.

What are your favorite ways to renew your soul?

_____

_____

_____

9. Double Up

Learn what tasks you can merge with others for optimum use of your time. (This is different from multitasking, which causes your brain to switch back and forth from one job to another, ultimately wasting time.)

Ways to double up:

◊ Combine two jobs, making sure that one of the jobs requires little thought.

◊ Use commuting time to pray or memorize Scripture.

◊   Keep a notebook with you to snatch time to write while waiting in line.

List a few ideas for doubling up that you've not tried, but would like to:

_____

_____

_____

10. Diagram Your Plan

Develop a written mission statement and reasonable, measurable goals. Those who write down their goals are ninety percent more likely to meet them!

Ways to diagram your plan:

➤ Determine what God and you want from your writing: a few articles published, books, to make a living at writing, to touch lives, or all of the above.

➤ Put dates on your goals—make them attainable and measurable.

➤ Use day-planners, white boards, and online tools.

List three attainable, measurable goals with dates that you'd like to accomplish:

_____

_____

_____

Chapter 3
Minutes Count

You have only a few minutes before you zoom out the door for your child's recital, a lunch meeting, or your day job. In the past, you may have thought you needed large chunks of time to work at writing and its related tasks. But if you'll allow yourself to think in terms of nibbles rather than gulps, you'll be surprised at how much you can accomplish. Here are some examples of what you can achieve in these little snacks of time.

Five Things to Complete in Five Minutes

1. Pray for guidance, protection, our nation's leaders, your family, and your writing.

2. Grab a dictionary and learn a new word.

3. File a paper or two that are cluttering your desk.

4. Eat a high energy snack: nuts, cheese, or raw fruit.

5. Read a page or two of an instruction book.

Ten Tasks to Accomplish in Ten Minutes

1. Revise one sentence or paragraph of your work in progress.

2. Write a thank you note or text message to an editor, fellow writer, or mentor who's inspired you.

3. Answer an e-mail or two.

4. Open God's Word and see what wisdom, love, or new ideas pop out as you meditate.

5. Journal a prayer for your writing, including what you believe God is speaking to you.

6. Clean off one bookshelf in your office, bagging books to give away.

7. Brainstorm ideas for a character, scene, or article.

8. Read a blog post and comment on it.

9. Post on Facebook©, Twitter©, or Pinterest© as a marketing tool.

10. Write the rough draft of a query letter to an agent or editor.

Chapter 4
Forty Time Management Tips and Secrets

Tips 1 to 20 apply specifically to writers
Tips 21 to 40 apply to everyone

1. Pray, asking the Lord to lead you on the unique writing/publishing path He wants you traveling on, where you'll be most fulfilled and successful. Follow His leading, not the leading of others. He is the Shepherd. They are fellow sheep.

2. Take a book with you everywhere. You can read while you wait in line at the post office or bank, for your food at a restaurant, even for rides at amusement parks!

3. Break chores down into baby steps. Satan would like to convince us we have to finish tasks in one sitting, so we'll get discouraged and never start. Every book, article, poem, and song began with the first sentence. Just start. (See the chapter entitled "Minutes Count.")

4. Keep your e-mail inbox tidy. Move messages you want to save or look at later to folders. Answer and delete others. If you find you're always de-

leting certain messages from particular senders, unsubscribe from them.

5. Keep a twenty-four-hour cyber Sabbath, staying off the Internet for a day each week. If you have a personality type that panics at the thought of being disconnected for an entire day, try unplugging for three hour stretches *every* day.

6. Limit TV watching to a few favorite shows. Don't just watch—analyze to become a better writer. What plot line, characterization, and dialogue works, and what doesn't? Keep a notebook handy so you can jot down inspired thoughts, and then apply those to your writing.

7. Never wait until the last minute—something will always come up to delay your finishing on time. Allow plenty of margin for interruptions and glitches. If your deadline is August 14th, have August 1st as your personal finishing goal.

8. Keep a notebook or digital recorder with you so you can write down ideas as they come. This includes your bedside table. Some of the richest ideas come at night when your mind is relaxed.

9. Keep your goals in a visible place—if you see them often, you're more likely to accomplish them.

10. Put encouraging Scriptures, soothing paintings, and inspiring quotes on the wall above your keyboard, where you'll see them constantly. If your personality needs variety, change them often to keep the muse fresh.

11. Reward yourself when you finish a less than enjoyable task.

12. If you wrestle with the discipline of keeping your backside in the chair to write, set the timer for fifteen minutes, thirty minutes, or an hour. Don't stop writing until it dings. You might surprise yourself when the ideas flow so well that you don't hear the bell, and you continue writing well past the timer's end.

13. Make your goals realistic and measurable. Put dates on them, so you can check off or erase them when you reach them. Share them with others who will hold you accountable.

14. Know your distracters, so you can avoid or manage them. Mute your phone and e-mail notification. Put a "Do Not Disturb" sign on your office door. Go to the library, café or park—whatever it takes to get the muse flowing. Some writers even travel to a secluded spot away from home so they can take several days or a week to concentrate on writing without interruptions. One famous novelist works in a bare room on a computer with no Internet access.

15. If a large job is stressing you, walk away for a bit and do something different—take a short walk, work in the garden, read a chapter of a novel— then come back to the task. You'll be more productive if your brain has a break.

16. Don't underestimate the power of five, ten, or fifteen minutes of work to whittle away at a huge project. Even God created the universe in increments. He is able and willing to help you create your masterpiece in small chunks.

17. As a seed, give some time helping another writer succeed. This could mean posting a book review, interviewing him or her for a blog post, or offering free editing advice. Expect the Lord to give you a harvest of time to write.

18. Be accountable to someone you trust. Say, "I will start the article for *Messy Moms Magazine* by _____." Ask that person to call or e-mail you to make sure you followed through.

19. Ask yourself, "If I had time to do only *one* thing on my list, what would I do?"

20. Simplify your environment. Clutter care wastes hours a week. Trying to find something in a stack, dusting endless knickknacks, picking up and putting away oodles of stuff—it all uses time you could be spending writing or reading. Be ruthless with yourself about how many possessions you keep. Riches are best when used as tools, not tyrants.

21. Make meals in large batches and freeze some for a later occasion when you don't have time to prepare a meal.

22. Hire someone to clean house, do yard work, babysit, run errands, and/or cook.

23. Choose tomorrow's outfit tonight. For extra busy weeks, choose seven outfits on Sunday night.

24. Use TV and phone time to do mindless chores—fold clothes, put clean dishes away, clean out a drawer, sign books, sew loose buttons, etc.

25. Use paper plates, cups, and plasticware to save time washing dishes. Even when having guests for a meal, you can compliment them by saying, "I'd rather visit with you than wash dishes. Do you mind the paper plates?" If they say, "Yes, I do mind," never invite them back!

26. Don't buy clothes that need to be dry cleaned. Or, use a do-it-yourself dry cleaning kit, which saves both money and time.

27. Listen to lively music while doing housework. It will help you move faster.

28. Don't spend large amounts of time with negative or lazy people. They'll bring you down and hinder you from reaching your God-given dreams and goals. If you're married to or work with this type of person, detox your thinking with much prayer, Scripture meditation, and listening to worship music.

29. Learn to say no without apologizing. Love and respect yourself enough to set boundaries on your time and energies.

30. Always put your keys in the same place. If that's too tough for your personality style, keep an ex-

tra set of house keys with a neighbor or hidden outdoors. An extra car key can go on a separate key chain that you carry with you at all times. But ladies, don't keep it in your purse. If you lock your purse in the car, that key will mock you while you're calling the locksmith.

31. Organize your closet, either by type of garment or color. This will streamline choosing an outfit. Once or twice a year, get rid of clothes you haven't worn in twelve months, or choose to give away clothes simply to bless someone else. When you buy new garments, give away the same number of clothes you purchased.

32. Exercise for high energy. The best way is to find a sport or strenuous activity you enjoy, and do it regularly. Park far from store entrances, to make yourself walk, unless it's after dark. Use the stairs instead of the elevator. To burn more calories, do tasks standing up instead of sitting.

33. Laugh frequently. Discover what makes you laugh, and do that often. Hang around witty people, watch comedy movies, or read books you find funny. Laughter releases the same endorphins exercise does, so it keeps you healthy and relieves stress.

34. Pray instead of complaining. Griping weakens you and slows you down, both physically and mentally.

35. Do your least desirable chore first to get it out of the way. Save your most appealing tasks for last.

36. Overcome fear by using God's Word and prayer— worry is a huge time waster.

37. When walking from one room to another, take something with you to put away. This adds mere seconds to your travel time, but saves huge chunks of time cleaning off an entire countertop or table.

38. Instead of selling unwanted items at yard sales, give away your past treasures. To save even more time, don't catalogue it for taxes—simply plant it as a seed, and expect God to bless you in return.

39. Ask the Lord to reveal to you what deeper need in your life is overriding the need to organize and manage your time wisely. Be willing to receive His love and forgiveness for past sins or wounds that might be causing confusion or passivity.

40. Choose friends who are enthusiastic about your goals and will encourage you. Make time to meet with them regularly.

Chapter 5
Confessions of a
Clutter Hypocrite

I planned to include a chapter about keeping clutter at a minimum as a way to manage time. But then I looked around my office and saw piles of papers and books on my desk, three inboxes full of files, and a bulletin board showing very little cork. In the dining room, the backs of chairs serve as shirt hangers, and cat toys litter the floor. Bibles, journals, and books jostle for position on my loveseat. It's the same with the counter in my bathroom—at least three books are stacked there at any given time.

So I can't write this chapter, because I am a clutter hypocrite. But if I did write it, I'd tell you that:

◊   Clutter complicates not only our environments, but also our lives, distracting us from doing what God has called us to do.

◊   When we own too much junk, we become slaves to our possessions. They go from tools to tyrants, demanding time to clean, organize, file, and put away.

◊   If we measure the value of things by how much they benefit us in relation to the time and effort we give them, we can identify clutter vs. treasures.

◊   Lasting happiness springs from loving, healthy relationships—with God and others. Caring for, sorting, and tripping over a huge collection of things depletes our spiritual and emotional energy we could be spending on relationships.

◊   It's easier to play "pick up sticks" than "let's clean up the forest." If we spend a bit of time every day putting or throwing things away, huge de-junking sessions won't be necessary.

I'd also suggest that if you realize your home and/or office is full of clutter, and you want to de-junk, you should start by getting rid of anything that:

◊   Is broken and not worth fixing,

◊   Is the wrong size, color, or style, and

◊   Is taking up more room, time, or money than the happiness it gives.

Then I'd tell you how to accomplish this:

◊   Enlist help from a trusted but objective friend who isn't as attached to your collection of hair bows from elementary school or scratched Elvis records. Spend a day together, de-junking everything that fits into the above three categories.

◊   Give, give, give to charities, homeless shelters, and thrift stores. Just don't give it to relatives who are likely to give it back to you, or a secondhand store where you frequently shop.

◊   Reward yourself after each room, drawer, or box
    you've cleaned out. But not with more stuff! Read
    a chapter from a novel, eat a favorite snack, or see
    a movie. Then revel in how much time you are
    freeing to write and focus on relationships.

But, alas, for the reasons mentioned earlier, I can't
write this chapter. I'd feel terrible if you read it, took
its advice, and then sent me an e-mail saying how
much more you're accomplishing since de-junking
your office and home. I'd be envious of your simpler
lifestyle and the extra time you had to spend writing.
That feeling might force me to call a friend and ask
her to help me de-junk, so I could gain more time.

Perhaps I should write it after all . . .

Chapter 6
Top Ten Time Thieves
That Attack Writers

*W*hen someone stole our credit card information, we canceled the card. But when time thieves break into my writing schedule and steal precious time, I shrug and say, "I'll do that project tomorrow." Too many of these robberies lead to unfinished projects and blocked goals.

Your time stealers may vary, depending on your personality. I imagine you can relate to at least some of these productivity robbers that regularly sneak up on me:

1. **Shallow chitchat.** Long conversations about meaningless topics—whether in person, on the phone, or online—rob my creative energies. I don't mean the person on the other end of the conversation is always the chatty one!

2. **Checking e-mails than more twice a day.** Yes, I'm eager to see if that editor bought my article or offered me a book contract, but I'm not *so* important I can't wait a few hours to find out. Constantly checking my inbox interrupts the flow of ideas.

3. **Unrestrained time on social networking sites**. Because I'm a people person, Facebook© and Pinterest© can purloin huge chunks of my time. Before I know it, ten minutes have turned to thirty. Unless I'm using these sites to market my book or brand, I end up playing too long. Play is a good thing, but it can quickly turn into a time waster.

4. **Answering the phone during writing time.** If I don't monitor calls, I lose my momentum, and then it takes time to get back into the muse.

5. **Arguing, fussing, and fighting**. Of course, we need to discuss why he thinks I shouldn't quit my day job yet, and why I think I should've quit yesterday. But when discussions lead to strife, it may take me hours to recover my composure enough to write a decent sentence.

6. **Distractions.** I walk into the kitchen to get a drink of water. I see cat bowls on the floor and pause to put them in the sink. I realize an eggshell left from breakfast needs to go down the disposal. While it's grinding I look out the window and notice the glider, which needs to be put away before cold weather comes. I pop outside, etc., etc., etc. Too many of these impulse activities and I've lost a huge chunk of productive time.

7. **Taking care of clutter and possessions.** As we discussed in a previous chapter (that I didn't write), the more I own, the more maintenance my stuff requires. If I de-clutter on a regular basis, I think more clearly and create more.

8. **Saying "yes" when I should say "no"** to tasks and activities the Lord never called me to do. Again, my people-pleasing style comes into play. I think I'll be making others happy if I say "yes." I'm really spreading myself too thin, which leads to mediocre writing, or not enough time to write.

9. **Not delegating**. If I try to do everything myself, I don't give others the opportunity to help. I also become crabby from overwork and stress, and my muse languishes.

10. **Negative emotions**. I waste more time than I care to admit on anger, frustration, and despair. When I yield to these thieves, they steal my joy and squelch my ideas. Thankfully, I'm learning to resist them in Jesus' name, and kick them out of my brain and my day!

Chapter 7
Ask an Expert

*D*o you ever wonder how expert writers and editors manage their time? You might be surprised at some of their answers.

From Cecil Murphey:

"Occasionally I have tasks that don't demand immediate attention, I don't like doing them, or I'm not sure what to do.

"For example, recently *Significant Living* magazine asked me to write an 800-word article for them on generous giving. Although I said 'yes,' I had no idea what I wanted to write. The publisher gave me six weeks to get the article to them. That made it one of those 'I can delay' tasks.

"On a lined, yellow pad, along with other non-urgent items, I wrote *Generous Giving*. Each day as I worked at my desk, I glanced at the list, but took no action. I consciously deferred thinking about any of them. (My unconscious mind, however, was working.)

"Before I handle any non-demanding tasks, I answer three questions.

1. *When do I need to have it finished?* I like to beat deadlines, so I decided I had four weeks to finish

the piece.

2. *How long do I expect the project to take?* Sometimes I only need to fill out forms with tedious questions. In creative writing, I have to allow for the ruminating process before I can write or complete needed research.

    "I'm a fast writer, but I needed time to think about the topic of giving. In free moments over the next couple of weeks, I thought about the article, and wanted to write one that didn't sound like a dozen others. One day while eating lunch, a title came to me: 'God Doesn't Want Your Money.' It felt right. After that, random ideas began to flow, but I still didn't write anything.

3. *When will I start?* That is the most important of the three questions. The day I received the assignment, I wrote the starting date on my yellow pad.

    "I'd never written for that magazine before and wanted to be sure I gave them what they wanted. If it didn't fit their needs, I wanted them to let me make changes and still beat the deadline.

    "By having a definite starting date, I programmed myself toward doing the task. I wrote and edited the article in one day, left it overnight, edited it again, and sent it to my proofreader.

    "In this case, I sent the article to *Significant Living* three weeks before it was due. Two days later, I received an e-mail from the editor with one word: *'perfect.'* (Cecil Murphey, author or co-author of 135 books including international best sellers such as *90 Minutes in Heaven* (with Don Piper); *Gifted Hands: The Ben Carson Story.* He has published 1,100 articles. www.cecilmurphey. com)

Diana Flegal says, "Read. Ignore e-mails, and stay off Facebook© and Pinterest©. I have to work from a "to-do list." (Diana Flegal, Agent, Hartline Literary, http://hartlineliteraryagency. blogspot.com)

Here's Bob Hostetler's best tip:

"My best technique or strategy is an old one, ancient even: Morning prayer. Praying before I start work organizes my day for me, sets (and sometimes utterly rearranges) my priorities, and saves me from the tendency I have to think and act as if I must accomplish everything alone.

"The other thing that comes to mind immediately is this: I use reminders and alerts on my iPhone® and computer, but they have not replaced an analog tool that has helped me make the most of my time and efforts: a "bring up" file (sometimes called a "tickler file") comprised of forty-three folders—twelve labeled with the names of the months and the rest numbered one through thirty-one. Every morning I pull out that day's numbered folder, which will contain any paperwork remaining from the previous day (allowing me to start every day with a clean desk, by the way), hotel or airline reservations, birthday cards to send, bills to be paid, and so on. On the first of each month, then the contents I've been filing away to remember during that month will be divided up into the thirty-one numbered folders, and the process begins again. It's easily the best mnemonic and time management tool I've ever used. I rely on it." (Bob Hostetler, award-winning writer, editor, pastor, and speaker. His twenty-six books, which include *The Bone Box* and *American Idols,* have sold millions of copies. He has co-authored eleven books with Josh McDowell, including the best selling *Right from Wrong* and the award-winning *Don't Check Your Brains at the Door.* He has won two Gold Medallion Awards, three Ohio Associated Press awards, and an Amy Foundation Award, among others. www. bobhostetler.com)

This is Diana Savage's strategy:

"When I'm busy shaping sentences, creating characters, and pondering plots, I often give no thought to such trivia as paying bills and keeping medical appointments. So my top two secrets to time management are 1) to-do lists, and 2) kitchen timers.

"On paper I write important upcoming tasks and put the list by my keyboard. Instead of juggling the items in my head while trying to write, I simply glance at the paper to see what needs to be done when I take breaks. (Keeping computer lists doesn't work for me.)

"Kitchen timers—the kind that won't stop buzzing until I get up and turn them off—pull me out of the literary world I'm creating so I can start dinner, make calls, and get ready for meetings. These tools allow me to give free reign to my creativity instead of diluting my concentration with self-micromanagement." (Diana Savage, author or co-author of ten books including *52 Heart Lifters for Difficult Times* and more than one hundred articles, editor, minister, and the principal at Savage Creative Services. www.DianaSavage.com)

Here is Jim Watkins's contribution, explained in his inimitable style:

"There are many famous formulas: $E=MC^2$ has something to do with the speed that traffic lights change relative to how far you have to travel and how late you are. $C=PiR$, if I remember correctly, is helpful in cutting a pie into even portions. Of course, there's Formula 409®, which I have never seriously tried to master.

"Here's another formula—and you don't need a pocket protector full of engineering pens to understand it: **YZ > A R = C**

"Simply put, if the amount **your zeal (YZ)** is greater than your **area of responsibility (AR)**, then you will experience **composure (C)**.

For instance, Kevin has the zeal and energy of the Energizer Bunny® on speed, so let's say he has ten "Z-factors" for his amount of energy and zeal (YZ). He's married, a father of two, works sixty-plus hours per week as a nuclear power operator, and serves as a member of the county school board for a score of "eight" for "areas of responsibility" (AR). As long as his amount of zeal (ten) is greater than his areas of responsibility (eight), he will experience "composure."

"Let's say that Elizabeth is a working mom with two preschoolers, volunteers at the local Crisis Pregnancy Center, and is guardian of her aging parents, so also has an eight for areas of responsibility. But—uh oh—her "Z-factor" is only a seven. Because her amount of zeal (YZ) is less than her area of responsibility (AR), the YZ >AR = C equation is reversed and, instead of composure (C), she feels like she's going . . . **C = R A>Z Y**

The "Z-Factor Theory," then, is quite simple. If we're going to maintain composure in our lives—and avoid being ordered to see a court-appointed psychiatrist—our energy level needs to be greater than our areas of responsibility.

"It is possible to increase our energy by eating right, exercising, and taking our vitamins every morning. But until we look like the Greek gods or goddesses on those workout videos, we may need to try something less Olympian. (James N.

Watkins, author or contributor of thirty books and two thousand articles, editor, instructor at Taylor University, conference speaker, minister, humorist, and "threat to society." www. jameswatkins.com)

Jody Hedlund says, "Take full advantage of writing time. When you get a block of concentrated writing time, don't respond to e-mails. Don't write blog posts. Don't answer interviews. Don't go on Facebook©. Don't do any work except *writing*." (Jody Hedlund, best-selling romance novelist of *The Preacher's Bride*, *The Doctor's Lady, Unending Devotion*, and *A Noble Groom.* http://jodyhedlund.com)

Marsha Hubler adds, "I always tell beginning writers there is no such thing as wasted time. You can write if you are in a doctor's waiting room, in line at the grocery store, or riding in the car; ninety percent of good writing is thinking. Think through your story often, and it will be easier to actually write." (Marsha Hubler, best-selling author of the *Keystone Stables* series and the *Loves of Snyder County* Amish/Mennonite series. www. marshahubler.com)

Prolific author Doc Hensley advises, "Always strive for closure on projects. You don't get praised or paid for only one act of a three-act play or only the first six chapters of a twenty-eight-chapter novel. People who have parts of manuscripts scattered all over their offices are not writers.

They are people who play at being a writer. Real writers finish one project and then market it and then move on to the next project." (Dr. Dennis E. Hensley, Director of the Professional Writing Department at Taylor University, author of 3,500 articles, 150 short stories, and 54 books, including *How to Manage Your Time* (Warner Press) and *Jesus in the 9 to 5* (AMG). www.dochensley.com)

Linda Glaz says, "Jeanette, I think the most important thing we can all do to stay focused on our writing is to avoid the trap of social media. Playing games on Facebook© doesn't help the word count. Establish set times each day for play time as breaks and the rest for writing. Do not be tempted." (Linda S. Glaz, Author and Agent, Hartline Literary Agency, http://lindaglaz.blogspot.com, http://hartlineliteraryagency.blogspot.com)

Here is Christine Lindberg's advice:

"My default for success in anything, including time management, is "PGF": Put God First. (Explanation: Any work I do without the Lord's blessing is largely a waste of time, so I precede every session of work with a prayer for guidance, focus, and productivity. Invariably, I am able to do more (and better) work in a single hour blessed by God than in a whole day on my own.

"If you are a writer or editor who works independently from your home, there are four rules you need to be aware of:

"Rule #1. Most people do not consider the

work you do a "real job," and therefore do not consider your work time inviolable.

"Rule #2. Your work time *is* inviolable.

"Rule #3. You can't change Rule #1, so you have to be in control of Rule #2. That means answering no personal phone calls or e-mail during your working hours. If necessary, it may also mean posting a notice on your front door and/or the door to your workspace: "Writer [*or* Editor*]* is working. Unless there is an emergency, please come back later, leave a message at [*phone number*], or send an e-mail to [*address*]. Thank you."

"Rule #4. If you accept the blessing of being entitled to manage your own time and you follow Rule #3 accordingly, you will be amazed how quickly Rule #1 starts to fade." (Christine Lindberg, former lexicographer for 30 years with Oxford Press)

Bonnie Calhoun's tip is short and sweet: "Just do it. Discipline comes in many forms, and until you learn to stick to a schedule you will be lost." (Bonnie Calhoun, Author, Owner/publisher at *Christian Fiction Online Magazine*, Owner/ Director, Christian Fiction Blog Alliance. http:// bonniecalhoun.com)

Recommended Reading and Websites

Don Aslett. *Clutter's Last Stand* (Pocatello, ID: Marsh Creek Press, 2nd ed., 2005)

Marlene Bagnull. *Write His Answer* (Lansdale, PA: Ampelos Press, 3rd ed., 2014)

Emilie Barnes and Sheri Torelli. *More Hours in My Day* (North Eugene, OR: Harvest House Publishers, 2008)

Dennis E. Hensley. *How to Manage Your Time* (New York: Warner Books, 1990)

Nadine Hill. *I Don't Have Time to Write!*

Charles E. Hummel. *Tyranny of the Urgent* (Downers Grove, IL: IVP Books, 1994)

Joyce Meyer. *100 Ways to Simplify Your Life* (Nashville, TN: FaithWords, 2008)

Susan Titus Osborn. *"How Do You Find Time to Write?" in Just Write! An Essential Guide for*

Launching Your Writing Career (Fullerton, CA: The Christian Communicator, 2009)

Mark Porter. *The Time of Your Life* (Overland Park, KS: Walterick Publishing Ministries, Inc., 2nd ed. 1988)

Works Cited

Aslett, Don. *Clutter's Last Stand.* Writer's Digest Books, www.writersdigest.com, 1984.

LaHaye, Tim. *Spirit-Controlled Temperament.* Carol Stream, Illinois: Tyndale House, 1966, 1992.

Littauer, Florence. *Personality Plus.* Grand Rapids, Michigan: Revell, 1992.